D1321448

PEANUTS

FOR THE

SOUL

Published in Great Britain in 2017 by Canongate Books Ltd,
14 High Street, Edinburgh EH1 1TE

www.canongate.co.uk

1

Copyright © Peanuts Worldwide LLC, 2017

The moral right of the author has been asserted

British Library Cataloguing-in-Publication Data
A catalogue record for this book is available on
request from the British Library

ISBN 978 1 78689 069 6

PEANUTS written and drawn by Charles M. Schulz
Edited by Martin Toseland
Layout by Stuart Polson

Printed and bound in Great Britain by Clays Ltd, St Ives plc.

FSC

PEANUTS

FOR THE

SOUL

by Charles M. Schulz

CANONGATE

Contents

CHAPTER ONE
LIFE

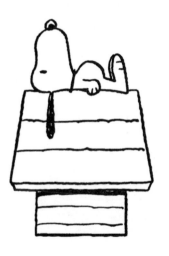

IT'S SO SAD..EVENTUALLY EVERYTHING IN LIFE JUST BECOMES ROUTINE..

HE SAID, "I'VE LEARNED THAT EVEN WHEN PEOPLE ASK ME THAT QUESTION, THEY AREN'T GOING TO LISTEN!"

CHAPTER TWO
LOVE

Dear Sweetheart,
I treasure your
last letter.

I have read it
over and over. It
made me so happy.

Only one little
part bothered me...

Where you misspelled
my name.

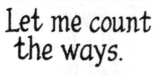

ALTHOUGH, IN THE LONG RUN, IT ALSO COULD SAVE YOU A LOT OF TROUBLE...

CHAPTER THREE
FAMILY

CHAPTER FOUR
FRIENDSHIP

Dear Little Red-Haired Girl, I don't have enough money to take you out to dinner.

A friend of mine suggested that maybe you'd enjoy just standing on a corner eating an orange.

AND THEN, GUESS WHAT, CHUCK..THIS KID CALLED ME "GOLF BALL NOSE"

SO I FIGURED YOU KNOW WHAT IT'S LIKE BEING CALLED NAMES ALL THE TIME BECAUSE YOU'RE SO INEPT AND EVERYTHING..

AND THAT'S WHY I CALLED, CHUCK, AND YOU'VE MADE ME FEEL A LOT BETTER... THANKS, CHUCK..

CHAPTER FIVE

BACK TO SCHOOL

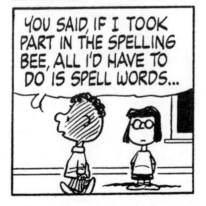

MAYBE I CAN THINK
OF SOMETHING ELSE...

CHAPTER SIX
AT PLAY

CHAPTER SEVEN
HAPPINESS

AND IT SAYS THAT ALTHOUGH HE HAD
NEVER SEEMED HAPPY, AND NO ONE RE